Love Stuff

Love Stuff

515 Delightful, Delicious, Sexy,
Silly, Fun, Frivolous, Passionate, Positive,
and (Above All) Romantic Things to
Do with Your One-and-Only

Lorraine Bodger

**Andrews McMeel
Publishing**

Kansas City

Love Stuff © 2004 by Lorraine Bodger. All rights reserved.
Printed in Canada. No part of this book may be used or
reproduced in any manner whatsoever without written
permission except in the case of reprints in the context
of reviews. For information, write Andrews McMeel
Publishing, an Andrews McMeel Universal company,
4520 Main Street, Kansas City, Missouri 64111.

04 05 06 07 08 TNS 10 9 8 7 6 5 4 3 2 1

ISBN: 0-7407-4680-4

Library of Congress Control Number: 2004101471

Illustrations by Lorraine Bodger
Book design by Lisa Martin

Introduction

$\mathcal{L}$ove and romance—two of the greatest thrills in the universe. When love walks in, each day is a delight. When romance is on your menu, you look forward to *everything*. Life is juicy, full of unexpected small pleasures—and large ones, too. You're roughly ten thousand times happier with yourself, your partner, and everyone else. Who in the world wouldn't want to keep love and romance going twenty-four hours a day, seven days a week?

But romance has a bad habit of disappearing just when you need it most. It sneaks away into laundry and dust bunnies and arguments and kids with runny noses, business trips and project deadlines and family visits, computer crashes and leaky faucets and car repairs. When life piles on the distractions, romance gets buried. And oh, how you miss it when it's gone!

How do you get it back? How do you retrieve that head-over-heels feeling? How do you and your partner even find *time* for romance? You find it when you say to yourselves, We need love and romance more than we need to mop the kitchen floor or plant rose bushes. More than we need to go to another soccer game. More than we need to stay late at the office. When you've straightened out your priorities, *then* you're ready to plan for romance, make room for it, embrace it.

And how do you light that fire again? You read *Love Stuff*, you choose romantic things to do, and *you do them. Thinking* about romance is great, but *making it happen* is much better. Keeping the romance in your romance requires *action. Action* is the operative word, and this kind of action is the most exciting kind—joyous and surprising and *fun.* This week you and your partner may only (only!) have time to snuggle on the couch at midnight, but next week, next month—anything goes!

Open a bottle of wine and settle in for a private talk about what sort of romance you'd like to get back into your life. Your personal choice might be plain or fancy, quiet or noisy, casual or formal, naughty or nice. It might be as simple as taking walks together at sunset or going dancing on the weekend, or as jazzy as season tickets to the opera or planning a round-the-world cruise. Or it might involve something a little sexier. Whatever it is, explore the possibilities (and thumb through the rest of *Love Stuff* for more ideas), and set a date and time for taking action.

Love Stuff

Pick a night and go to bed (together!) early.

Pick an afternoon and spend it
(together!) doing two or three favorite
things. Not *your* favorite things, not
his favorite things, but things that are
favorites of *both* of you.

Love Stuff

Pick a weekend and spend it (together!) in the nicest hotel, inn, or bed-and-breakfast you can afford. If you have kids, leave them with someone you trust completely and *do not call home even once.*

Pick a week and spend it (together!) in a place you've always wanted to visit. Doesn't matter if it's Tahiti or Cleveland as long as it's where you both want to be.

Love Stuff

6

Run a bath for her and add fragrant bath oil. Put a glass of chilled white wine where she can reach it easily from the tub. Light a few candles. Escort her into the bathroom, and lock the door if there's a chance someone else (like your ten-year-old) will barge in. Help her into the soothing hot water, then stay to chat until the bath starts to cool. Dry her off gently, and wrap her in her robe.

Keep Out! Bath in Progress

Love Stuff

7

Ask your partner to plan a special dinner menu, then make it for him and him alone. No guests, no kids—nobody but the two of you. Don't forget wine, candles, flowers, and a few perfect chocolates to top off the meal in a deliciously romantic way.

8

Find out more about each other: Take magazine quizzes together—not because they're reliable, but because your mate's answers will probably come as interesting surprises.

Get matching ID bracelets and have them engraved with each other's names. A little throwback to high school . . .

Make a (mutual) written commitment for six months of Saturday night dates.

Sit on his lap. Murmur in his ear. Snuggle.

Love Stuff

12

Buy a different pair of frivolous, sexy panties for each day of the week. Let him know.

13

Take lots of pictures of each other. What's more romantic than knowing your mate has his full attention on your adorable self through the lens of a camera? What's more romantic than knowing she wants to have a permanent memory of handsome, dashing you?

Love Stuff

14

And while we're on the subject of photos: Have a professional take photographs of the two of you together. Order and frame two copies of the best shot, one for your desk, one for hers. Look at the photo often and remember how much you love each other.

Love Stuff

What's more romantic than the night sky? That's easy: two lovers out under it!

♥ Learn the constellations and point them out to each other.

♥ Watch the Perseid meteor shower.

♥ Look for shooting stars and make wishes on them.

♥ Contemplate the harvest moon.

♥ Cuddle in a sleeping-bag-for-two as twilight turns to velvety darkness.

Give *him* a gift certificate from Victoria's Secret. No, you didn't read that wrong. Give him a gift certificate and let *him* pick out the lingerie he'd like you to wear. You may be in for a thrilling surprise.

And speaking of underwear, buy him some sexy bikini briefs. We're talking *really* hot here—black vinyl, black mesh, see-through. Browse online catalogs for the ones *you* like best.

Love Stuff

18

Fun and Games #1:
Challenge him to a game of hide-and-seek. If he's smart, he'll hide in a dark closet, in the attic, or anyplace else private—because when you find him . . .

19

Laughing together is joyous—and romantic—so do it as much as you can. Go to funny movies, watch TV comedies, check out hilarious video-tapes or DVDs from the humor section of your video store.

Love Stuff

20

Romantic Getaway:
Take a Baltic cruise and drop in on
Stockholm, Tallinn, Gdansk, or
St. Petersburg to explore.

21

Okay, so you don't love going to the
ballet and *she* doesn't love going to ice
hockey. Or vice versa. Is that any reason
not to go out together? Find something
(or several somethings) you *both* like
going out to see together, and do it (or
them) often.

22

Next time you have a dinner party, stand up and make a toast to your mate.

23

Give her an orchid or gardenia corsage, for no reason at all.

Love Stuff

24

Say NO when your darling suggests a night of romance: NO phone calls. NO pager. NO TV. NO kids. NO interruptions of any kind. Say YES to everything else.

25

Be appreciative—something we often forget in the hustle-bustle of an ordinary workday. But a word or two of gratitude is not only kind and thoughtful, it's romantic and loving as well, and your partner won't forget it. What goes around, comes around.

Love Stuff

26

Do some love stuff in unexpected places: Make love in a closet, a tent, the living room with the curtains wide open, the garden at night, a sleazy motel, a fancy hotel, someone else's bedroom. Kiss passionately behind a door at a wedding, a party, a formal dance. Caress each other under the table at a restaurant, behind the stacks in the library, in the stairwell at the office Christmas party. Have sex on the kitchen table, a fur rug, the beach, a waterbed, your desk. Tried all these hot spots? Invent a few more of your own.

Love Stuff

27

Love Stuff Project #1:

Get together over a large piece of heavy white paper and draw a beautiful, decorative family tree—his side, your side, yourselves, and your kids. Use colored markers, crayons, and maybe some glitter pens, too. Don't forget a fancy border!

28

Always exchange gifts on special occasions, even if the gifts are just small tokens.

Love Stuff

29

Take a morning coffee break together.

30

Rent a bicycle-built-for-two and take a ride.

31

Romantic Getaway:
Hit Rio de Janeiro for Carnivale. Dance till you drop.

Even if you're already married (to each other) you can still go out on a date as if you were courting. Let him pick you up at the door, dressed in his coolest outfit, bouquet in hand. Be waiting in your coolest outfit, freshly combed, scented, and hot to trot. And when he brings you home, invite him in for a nightcap.

Spend an enchanted romantic evening working on your mutual kissing techniques and give them the dedicated attention you'd give to improving your skill in any sport you love.

Day-trips are the perfect antidotes to short tempers and that general if-we-don't-have-some-fun-soon-I'm-going-to-strangle-the-cat feeling. So take a day off together and do *not* stay home. Get *away* from home as if you were taking a vacation. Get out into the country or drive into the city. Get yourself a thousand mental miles away from your usual routine, and you'll feel a thousand times more romantic.

35

On a hot summer day, turn the hose
on your sweetie to cool him off.

36

On a hot summer day, take a cool
shower together.

On a hot summer day, retire from the world behind closed curtains.

Give a birthday bash for your beloved, and make the main event a slide-show-plus-commentary all about him. Have his friends tell (flattering!) stories and anecdotes, too.

Instead of getting angry and frantic when you're stuck in traffic with your partner, change your attitude 100 percent. There you are, just the two of you, in a completely private space, and there's not a thing you can do to unsnarl the logjam. Why not relax and have a good time? Talk about the day's events. Sing together. Tell jokes. Play I-Spy. Hold hands. Plan your next vacation. Treasure this fortuitous gift of time together.

Shake a little hot pepper onto your relationship:

♥ Tell each other your favorite sexual fantasies.

♥ Make love at a time that's different from your usual hour of choice.

♥ Get naked and give each other full body massages.

♥ Read an erotic story together.

♥ Do all of the above, on different occasions.

41

Save your romantic gift for a rainy day:
Put twenty or thirty crisp one-dollar
bills inside your darling's umbrella,
close it carefully, and when she opens
it up—a shower of dollars for her to
spend on whatever she wants!

42

Tell him a secret from your past—not
something dire, but something funny
or silly or daring or wild. Make him tell
you one, too.

Love Stuff

43

Pretend you're a Boy Scout and be prepared. Make a list of all the parks, museums, galleries, movie theaters, and other fun places no more than an hour-and-a-half drive from your home. Make another list, of great restaurants within the same area. Make a third list, of farmers' markets, antique shops, bookstores, and other interesting shopping spots. Now you'll be ready to play when the impulse comes upon you and your partner. Pick a few things to do, hop in the car, and you're off to an adventure.

44

Bake him an angel food cake when he's being angelic. Bake him a devil's food cake when he's being devilish.

Love Stuff

45

Adopt a kitten or a puppy together.

46

Go to the gym and help each other with the machines.

47

Romantic Getaway:
Walk the Dolomites in northern Italy.

Love Stuff

48

Redecorate your bedroom and get a whole new perspective on romance. Move the furniture around. Change the lighting. Change the color scheme, perhaps from earth tones to bright tones or from pastels to jewel colors. You'll feel as if you're in a different world.

49

Love Stuff Project #2:
Restore a beautiful piece of furniture together.

Send your partner a bag of fortune cookies with wonderful messages.

Organize an old-fashioned autumn hayride for the two of you—or invite a few other romantically inclined couples to join you.

Hire a trio of musicians to serenade your love beneath her bedroom window on a starry night. And where are you while all this is happening? Singing softly in her ear.

When was the last time you necked in the last row of a movie theater? Take your partner to the flicks and do it.

54

Go out together for a walk in freshly fallen snow, first thing in the morning, before anyone else is awake—in a wood or park, on a country road or city street. Enjoy the silence, solitude, peace. Feel like the only two people left on the planet.

Love Stuff

55

Is there a wonderful hotel or inn you'd love to take your sweetheart to, but you've found it's impossible to make reservations unless you book months in advance? Great! Book a room *now* for Valentine's Day, her birthday, or your anniversary *next year*.

Love Stuff

56

A gift of flowers may be obvious, but that doesn't make it less desirable or romantic. How about one of these?

- ♥ a whole flat of pansies or a lushly flowering houseplant

- ♥ a dozen pale peach tea roses or six stems of fragrant lilies

- ♥ three or four birds of paradise in a tall glass vase

- ♥ a bouquet of wildflowers or a nosegay of assorted blooms in her favorite color

Your partner is special. He's one-of-a-kind. The romance gurus may tell you to wine and dine him at Le Restaurant Haute Cuisine, but if he doesn't drink, is on a diet, and loves to slop around in sweatpants—why would you take him there? Instead, stop and think. What kind of romancing would send *your* partner over the moon?

Have a midnight snack together.

Love Stuff

59

Next time you go shopping together, whether it's a trip to the supermarket, the Chic Boutique, the MegaCD Store, or the garden center, listen carefully to what your mate longs to have—then buy it for her when she's not looking.

60

Get yourselves some really comfortable patio furniture so you can spend romantic spring and summer evenings watching the sun go down or sitting under the stars.

Love Stuff

61

Cuddle for an entire evening (morning, afternoon) for the sheer pleasure of cuddling. Snuggle up together wherever you're super-comfortable, and be warm and cozy. If the cuddling leads to love-making, that's great; if not, you'll still be glowing from the intimacy.

62

Stroll hand-in-hand on a sugar-soft beach at sunrise.

Love Stuff

63

Arrange to meet her at the bar in the Hotel Splendide. Lurk behind a potted palm until you see her get comfortable on a bar stool and glance impatiently at her watch. Then secretly send the bartender over with her favorite cocktail and have him tell her it's from an admirer. Sidle over and . . . pick her up.

Love Stuff

64

Spend a week in London and go to a
romantic play, comedy, or musical
every single night. Then head up to
Stratford-on-Avon for some romantic
Shakespeare.

65

Put up a corkboard or a small black-
board and leave romantic notes for
each other—often.

Love Stuff

66

Write him a book: Buy a handsome album and fill it with stories, photos, poems, quotes, mementos, and anything else you think he'd enjoy.

67

Play hooky from work together for a whole day. Plan ahead (be sure the kids have somewhere safe to go after school and for dinner), but don't try to decide ahead of time how you and your sweetie will spend those precious hours with each other. See how it plays out.

Love Stuff

68

Sit down and have a heart-to-heart about whatever gets in the way of your being romantic. Is it the constant demands of a new baby? Your fear of intimacy? Exhaustion from overwork at your job? Worries about money? The example your parents set for you? Try to be honest, and try *not* to be defensive. Be gentle and understanding. See if you can find ways of overcoming the problems, either by yourselves or with professional help.

CDs, CDs, CDs: Give her a romantic disc every day for a week. Buy yourselves a CD of a great singer crooning great love songs. Treat yourselves to half a dozen of your mutual favorites, whatever the music category. But the real romance comes later: Listen to them together. Dance to them. Smooch on the couch while you're listening. Play them while you're making love.

Love Stuff

70

Take him to lunch at his usual hangout. Dress beautifully and let all his buddies see what a prize he's captured.

71

Flirt with her at a party. Seduce her when you get home.

72

Before you make love, smooth some flavored body lotion on a few strategic spots.

Love Stuff

73

Romantic Getaway:

Sail the Greek islands in the Aegean Sea in a rented sailboat with captain and crew.

74

Make hot buttered rum toddies on cold winter nights: In a heatproof pitcher combine two jiggers of dark rum, a twist of lemon peel, a clove, and a cinnamon stick. Add boiling cider to taste (enough for two toddies), pour into mugs, and float a pat of butter on each.

Passion is infectious, and not just the kind of passion that happens behind closed doors. Be a more passionate person—start doing the thing you've always loved doing, whether it's cooking or bowling or playing the drums. Your passion will animate not only you but your relationship as well.

Send loving thank-you notes to each other to express your appreciation for gifts, for acts of thoughtfulness, for help given, and for just being there.

What's his favorite childhood lullaby?
Sing him to sleep with it.

"Romantic" means different things to
different people. Do you know what it
means to you? Do you know what it
means to your mate? Ask. You need to
know, because you don't want to make
him a present of the cute stuffed animal
that you think is romantic when he
actually thinks stuffed animals are . . .
well . . . dumb.

Love Stuff

79

Try aromatherapy with your darling.
Experiment to find the scents that put
you in your romantic mood of choice—
peaceful, calm, relaxed, or loving.

80

You're tearing around, working, cleaning,
fixing, helping, shopping, driving—*SLOW
DOWN*. Both of you have to stop what
you're doing. Sit on the
couch and relax. Hold
hands. Be together
instead of being apart.

Nothing, but nothing, is more romantic than being listened to with attention, respect, interest, compassion, and love. Try listening—really listening—to your sweetheart tonight.

82

Don't let stormy weather get in the way of romance. If it's raining (and raining and raining) make it a point to have a good time together anyway. Get out and go—to the movies, museum, mall, concert, dance club. Bowl, play pool, take an indoor swim. Of course, you *could* use the downpour as an excuse to stay in bed. Make rainy days into days you actually look forward to.

Love Stuff

Give your darling a ring—on the phone. Ask him out for a special night to re-create the best date you two ever had. Do not expect it to be the same as the first time; expect it to be even better.

Give your darling a ring—a real one. It could be a new wedding ring, a ring made of interlocking bands, a ring with a pretty stone, even a friendship ring. Be sure to include a note telling her what the ring says about your feelings.

Love Stuff

85

Love Stuff Project #3:

Design a Memory Wall. Frame lots of things that have special meaning for you and your mate—photos, your wedding invitation, a poster from a favorite romantic movie, and anything else. Arrange and hang on a freshly painted wall.

86

At holiday time, send your lover a huge basket of gourmet goodies—and he'd better share with you!

Prepare a duet, complete with perfect harmony, to perform at the very next anniversary party you're invited to.

Romantic Getaway:
Visit the famed Butchart Gardens on Vancouver Island, British Columbia, Canada.

Love Stuff

Put together a romantic weekend kit: scented soap, massage oil, bubble bath, candles, CDs, and above all, a DO NOT DISTURB sign. Tuck everything into a nice tote and present it to your mate. The two of you can scoot out of town with your kit if you want to, but you *could* just hang the D.N.D. sign on the front door and . . . stay home.

What's your daily departure routine? Do you gulp down your coffee while you're putting on your coat? Grab your briefcase and yell good-bye to your partner as you dash out the door? Not good enough. Stop right there. Find an extra three minutes (how hard is it to get up three minutes earlier?) to exit in a way that leaves both of you feeling good. Take a moment to hug and kiss good-bye. Promise you'll call during the day (and do it). Tell your dear one you're looking forward to a happy reunion at dinnertime. Now you're ready to leave. Wave as you drive off, and blow another kiss.

What's your daily arrival routine? Do you drag in with a frown on your face? Hang up your coat without a word of greeting and then escape to the den or the kitchen? Do you yell at the kids to be quiet? Not good enough. Stop and take a deep breath *before* you open the front door. You're glad to be home at last, and you've got to show it. Take a moment to give your mate a hug. Sit down and chat for five minutes (how hard is it to take five?). Change your clothes so you're more comfortable, and then proceed to the next activity in a calm, loving frame of mind. Now you've really arrived.

Love Stuff

92

Keep a bottle of champagne ready and waiting at the back of the fridge—for any occasion you can dream up. Don't wait for a conventional celebration day; drink it any time the two of you want to celebrate your happiness with each other.

93

Romantic Getaway:
Head south to Cabo San Lucas in Baja California.

Love Stuff

94

Spend an entire afternoon together at a day spa.

95

Buy him an ice cream cake in his favorite flavors, with a loving message written on top.

Love Stuff

96

Kissing, kissing, and more kissing—now, *that's* romantic. So do a lot more of it

- ♥ in front of a flickering fire in the living room
- ♥ in the back hallway in the shadows
- ♥ in bed
- ♥ in stolen moments
- ♥ all of the above

97

Give him a double frame for his desk— your baby picture right beside his.

Love Stuff

Read articles about romance in men's and women's magazines, but read them *together*. You may get ideas, you may get laughs, you may even get mad, but you'll certainly open up the topic of romance in a new way.

Go around the world in eighty, ninety, or a hundred days.

100

Here's a list of deliciously romantic videos for you to watch together: *Moonstruck; Enchanted April; Notting Hill; The Wedding Planner; Sleepless in Seattle; An Affair to Remember; The African Queen; Gone with the Wind; Sense and Sensibility; Shakespeare in Love; Sabrina; When Harry Met Sally; Truly, Madly, Deeply; The Big Easy; As Good as It Gets; Bridget Jones's Diary; Titanic; Only the Lonely.*

Love Stuff

❤ 101

Fun and Games #2:

Send your lover on a short treasure hunt—half a dozen clues that lead from one place to another and wind up at a special venue (restaurant, café, country inn, hotel) where you are waiting with champagne and kisses.

Is it any coincidence that _dance_ and _romance_ rhyme? If you two already love dancing together, make it a point to hit the dance floor often. If you're no Fred and Ginger, take lessons together and then never miss a chance to get out there and show what you can do.

Love Stuff

103

Give her a fitted-out picnic basket with all the bells and whistles—plates, glasses, flatware, food containers, tablecloth, napkins, and so on—and take her out for a fancy picnic.

104

Declare your romantic partnership: Have cocktail napkins, note cards, and memo pads printed with both your names.

Love Stuff

105

Ditch your watches (and turn the clocks to the wall) for a weekend. For forty-eight hours live solely *in* the moment and *for* the moment: Eat when you're hungry, sleep when you're tired, and do everything else exactly when you feel like it. Don't give a thought to WHEN; think only of WHAT and HOW and especially WHOM you're doing it with.

Fill your bedroom with candlelight and music. The light is flattering and the music you play can put you in your mood of choice: mellow and relaxed, soft and gentle, hot and exciting.

Fill your bedroom with fragrant flowers such as freesia or lilies, or with pine boughs or other spicy-smelling greens. Inhale deeply and luxuriate in the romantic transformation of your room.

108

Seduction is a part of love stuff and romance, too. Try this: Emerge from your hot, steamy shower wrapped in a towel, with only its corner tucked in to hold it on. Glide by your partner and see what happens next.

109

Dedicate a song to your honey, on the radio. (Make sure she's tuned in to hear it.)

Love Stuff

110

Send a giant box of his favorite chocolates—to his office.

111

Call him from your car, even if you've just left the house.

112

Take ice-dancing lessons together so you can glide over the ice doing turns and dips and jazzy steps. So-o-o romantic.

Love Stuff

113

Candlelight isn't just for dinner. Try it for breakfast in bed: Leave the drapes closed, light a dozen candles, and snuggle up together under the covers with a tray of goodies.

114

Drive the Alaskan Highway to Haines, Alaska, put your car on the ferry, and sail down to Seattle. Sit on deck and watch whales, eat great food, and stop off at romantic little villages.

115

What day of the week is hardest for your mate? Sunday, for instance, might be tough because it precedes the workweek or it reminds him of the old day-before-school syndrome. The cure for this problem is to *do* things instead of moping. Sunday is a great day for hiking and biking, for inviting the family over for a barbecue or having friends in for Sunday supper. Be *active*, not *passive*, and be active *together*. Sprinkle the day with love, too, in the form of hugs, kisses, and encouragement.

Love Stuff

116

Have a rendezvous: Leave work early and meet someplace romantic—a rooftop bar, a dimly lit restaurant, a café with a fireplace, a park bench, a rose garden.

Love Stuff

117

Lose your hearts to a fixer-upper dream house. As you restore it slowly, with care, you'll be partners in a very special kind of love affair.

118

Read a book that explains how to pin down and understand your personality types, to learn about your romantic inclinations.

119

Do small acts of love:

♥ Hide a tiny gift under her pillow.

♥ Give him a sheet of LOVE stamps.

♥ Tape a rose to her bathroom mirror.

♥ Feed him heart-shaped waffles.

Love Stuff

120

Do big acts of love:

♥ Buy her a complete new outfit,
  right down to the shoes.

♥ Give him twenty cans of tennis
  balls.

♥ Send her to a spa resort for a week
  of R & R.

♥ Help him do all of his clothes
  shopping.

Love Stuff

121

Pick a day, and for that one day deliver
a *barrage* of love notes by snail mail,
e-mail, and your own sweet hand.
More is better.

122

Be daring together: Go to a production
of experimental theater. Hear a concert
of experimental music. Look at an
exhibit of experimental art.

Love Stuff

123

No time for full body massages? Give each other soothing, relaxing face massages: Stroke lightly over the whole face, then firmly on forehead and cheeks, between the eyebrows, along the jaw line. Touch lips and ears gently. Finish up with plenty of kisses.

124

Watch TV with him when he's sick, so he won't feel lonely and anxious.

125

When you have to be apart for a week or two, agree to think of each other at exactly the same moment each day.

126

Next time you go on a business trip to an interesting city, take your partner along. Since your hotel room is already paid for, it's just a question of kicking in the extra plane fare—but try to stay an extra day or two for sightseeing and enjoying the city together.

Love Stuff

127

Decide on a special e-mail or phone message that alerts your partner to the fact that you've had the mother of all rough days. When either of you sends the message, the other one goes into caretaking mode: a glass of wine poured and waiting, dinner (or take-out Chinese), back rub, hot bath, peace and quiet—whatever it takes to restore your mate to sanity. Caretaking, when it's really meaningful, is loving and romantic.

128

Romantic Getaway:
Rent a cottage at Cinnamon Bay, on St. John, U.S. Virgin Islands.

129

Intimacy is romantic. Set a quiet time for the two of you to sit down and share your thoughts about your kids, your families, your work, your friends, even your problems.

Love Stuff

130

Have window boxes installed on your front windows and plant them with brightly colored flowers so that coming home each day will give her joy.

131

Surprise her with a gift certificate for a manicure and pedicure. Surprise him with a gift certificate for a massage.

Spend a day at a county or state fair. Check out the prize-winning tomatoes, blueberry pies, decorated cakes. Admire the cows, goats, fancy birds. Eat corn dogs, cotton candy, home-made fudge. Play a carnival game and win a giant stuffed animal for your sweetheart. Finish with a spin on the Ferris wheel, nestled together in the beautiful twilight.

Love Stuff

133

Give her a subscription to a romance book club to put her in the mood.

134

If you usually stay home on Sunday mornings with a toasted bagel and the Sunday paper, make a change: Go out for a wonderful brunch and eat something you'd never bother to cook at home—eggs Benedict, French toast, Belgian waffles.

Love Stuff

135

Routine is the bane of romance. If you do the very same thing day after day, night after night, your creative and romantic impulses are stifled with a capital S. You're probably bored silly— and you don't even know it! Time to make a change, starting *today*. Meet your mate after work for an outing to a movie, a snazzy bar, a concert, or museum. Have dinner at a charming café or restaurant. Take a walk or a bike ride, go for a swim or a sail. Get out of your rut and get romantic!

But here's the thing about getting out of your rut: Once is not enough. Those old habits are like paths worn into the floorboards: It takes more than one sanding to get rid of *them*. You've got to commit (if only in your own head) to repeating your daring act of romance (see item above), and—lest you tumble into another routine—you have to do something different *at least* every other week. No ifs, ands, or ruts.

137

Blue sky? Fresh breeze? Get out there and fly a pair of kites together.

Love Stuff

138

Make plans for a romantic summer: On Memorial Day, sit down together and make a list of fun things you'll do, from beach picnics to country walks, dinners under the stars to brunches by the shore, concerts in the open air to swing dancing under fairy lights.

139

Find a sidewalk caricaturist and have him draw your portraits, together.

Love Stuff

140

Buy a large journal, one that will lie open on a table. Leave it near the front door, with a pen resting conveniently in the center. Write notes to each other every day as you leave or arrive home, pass by, or simply remember something you meant to say. No need to write much—a wish or thought, a thank-you, a message of love or encouragement, anything that comes to mind and expresses your good (and romantic) feelings for your partner.

On the Fourth of July, go see the fireworks. And think about the fireworks you two can create when you get home.

Love Stuff Project #4:
Paint a mural on the playroom wall, depicting great moments and aspects of your relationship—your first date, your wedding, your honeymoon, your children, your first house, and so on.

143

If you're not used to calling your mate during the workday, *call!* Do it for a week and see how you like being in closer touch.

144

Make beautiful music together: *Sing!* Sing old favorites, new favorites, golden oldies, folk songs, opera, hymns, carols, ballads. Harmonize as only you two can.

Love Stuff

145

Sex, you may have noticed, can be an important part of kindling romance. Find more time for lovemaking, ASAP.

146

Have an outrageously indulgent meal that you cook together at home, throwing caution to the wind. Start with dessert, if that's what you crave! Hey, this could put you in such a happy mood that just about any deliciously romantic thing might happen when you finally leave the table.

Love Stuff

147

Leave her a gift where she's least expecting it, when she needs it most:

- ♥ on the rocking chair in the nursery, so she'll find it when she gets up at midnight to feed the baby

- ♥ wedged under the vacuum cleaner cord, so she'll come across it when she's stuck doing housecleaning

- ♥ on top of the washing machine, so she'll spot it when she lugs a load of clothes to the laundry room

- ♥ tucked into the toe of her running shoe, so she'll discover it when she's off for a hard run

Love Stuff

148

Do the old-fashioned honeymoon thing (even if it's not your real honeymoon): Visit Niagara Falls.

149

Whisk your guy away to a motel for the weekend—and arrange with the manager to have the sign outside the motel set up with a special love message. Try a nice straightforward SUSIE LOVES BOBBY, or BOBBY—MEET ME IN ROOM 301—LOVE, SUSIE.

150

To spend more time together, do an activity that happens *regularly*. If you take a class together, there you'll be, every Thursday at eight P.M. If you join the choir together, there you'll be at practice sessions every Tuesday evening at six. If you buy season tickets to the theater, there you'll be at the show every other Saturday night. And you'll have lots to talk about tête-à-tête over coffee afterward.

Love Stuff

151

If you're really daring, or at least not too shy, find a nude beach and take it all off.

152

Fun and Games #3:
Play footsie under the table. Keep a straight face no matter *what* happens down there.

Love Stuff

153

Hire a housekeeper for one afternoon per week and spend that afternoon together far, far away from the house and the housework.

154

Go to a street festival and browse the concessions for love stuff—scented oils, his-and-hers T-shirts, heart-shaped knickknacks. Share a smoothie, a shish kebab, a quesadilla.

Love Stuff

155

What's your idea of a perfect relationship? That's a trick question since no relationship is perfect, but play this little game anyway: Write a list of the qualities you envision in a perfect relationship. Exchange lists. How similar are they? Any changes you'd like to make in your current situation?

156

Romance each other with red: red satin sheets; spicy Zinfandel; American Beauty roses; cinnamon redhots to heat you up; raspberry tarts made with raspberries you pick together on a summer day; a visit to Muir Woods to see the giant redwoods; the red carpet rolled out for the two of you on a red-letter day—your anniversary.

Love Stuff

157

Romance each other with blue: blueberries and cream in bed on Sunday morning; flats of blue pansies and lobelia for your garden; a vacation in the Bluegrass region of Kentucky; his-and-hers blue-jean jackets embroidered with your names; a delicious dinner of bluefish, blue crabs, or bluepoint oysters; sapphire earrings or cufflinks; a bluebird of happiness in a bright blue sky.

158

Romance each other with green: juicy green grapes and pears; a vacation in Scotland on the golf greens; a night at home with a gallon of mint chocolate chip ice cream and a great video; melon liqueur martinis; four-leaf clovers for luck; a green light for love.

Love Stuff

159

Romance each other with pink: pink lightbulbs in the bedroom lamps; Pink Lady cocktails at a glamorous bar; matching pinky rings; Valentine's Day cake with cherry-pink frosting; bubble-gum; a pair of pink flamingos for the front yard; rose-colored glasses for an optimistic view of the world.

Love Stuff

160

Romance each other with yellow: yellowtail sushi at the best Japanese restaurant in town; a week at the Lake Yellowstone Hotel in Yellowstone National Park; banana splits at an old-fashioned ice cream parlor; bunches of daffodils all over the house; a walk in the rain in yellow slickers and yellow rubber boots; sweet lemonade made from real lemons.

Love Stuff

161

Wrap a tiny thrilling gift (a gem, a ring, the key to a new car, the key to your apartment, a pair of tickets to Spain, a pair of tickets to Wimbledon, a gold locket) in a small box and put the small box in a *huge* box, for a very romantic surprise.

162

Make a tape or CD of songs that express your feelings for your partner.

Love Stuff

163

Double-date with your oldest friends and tell stories about your courtships and weddings.

164

Oh, go ahead and take naughty pictures of each other! (Just be sure to keep them in a safe hiding place so the kids don't stumble onto them and feel duty-bound to take them to school for show-and-tell.)

If he's a chocoholic, give him a dozen Chocolate Coupons that entitle him to a variety of treats: homemade chocolate pudding; chocolates from his favorite candy shop; chocolate-flavored body paint; fudge sauce from a gourmet store; a chocolate malt at the local soda fountain; chocolate cake from his favorite bakery; chocolate mousse at a French café, and so on. Redeemable from you at any time he desires.

Love Stuff

166

Romantic Getaway:

Take a trip to Africa to stay in one of the lodges in Masai Mara National Reserve in Kenya or Serengeti National Park in Tanzania. Spend your days watching the amazing animals and your evenings having great food.

Love Stuff

167

Go to a good bookstore to find five paperbacks that you *both* want to read. Might be classics, humor books, the latest novels. Take turns reading and talking about them.

168

Decorate the house together at holiday time. Use lots of pine boughs and wreaths, plenty of twinkly lights and fat red candles, oceans of mistletoe.

Sending a love note? Have it delivered by bicycle messenger.

When you're out for drinks with friends, write your sweetheart a love note on one of the little paper cocktail napkins and slide it over to him when no one is looking.

Love Stuff

171

If your home is not a refuge for the two of you, how can you possibly get into a romantic mood? Improve your living conditions immediately! Set up a schedule for cleaning up, straightening up, replacing whatever isn't working or looks ugly, redecorating where possible. Turn your nest into a sanctuary from the outside world.

172

Lists, lists, lists! They're fun to write and fun to read. Here are a few romantic lists for you and your darling to write and exchange:

- ♥ Ten Things I Adore About You
- ♥ Ten Reasons I Fell for You
- ♥ Ten Things I Love About Making Love with You
- ♥ Ten Reasons Why We're Such Good Friends
- ♥ Ten Ways You Bring Me Joy

Love Stuff

173

Travel to someplace totally unexpected. For some folks it might be Iceland or Tierra del Fuego, for others it might be La Push, Washington, or Washington, D.C. It doesn't matter how exotic it is as long as it's an unexpected place for you to visit.

Love Stuff

174

Love those glamorous black-and-white Hollywood films of the 1930s? You and your leading man might like to scour vintage clothing stores for costumes— a marabou-trimmed satin negligee? A velvet smoking jacket? Dress up and do a little role-playing.

Love Stuff

175

Coming down with the flu (or a cold or cramps or back problems) is anything but romantic, but it is romantic and kind to lavish TLC on someone who's feeling sick: Make sure your partner is warm and comfortable. Bring a tray artfully laid out with tempting things to eat. Supply her with tissues, aspirin, an ice pack, a heating pad. Keep the kids away and the noise level down. Do whatever it takes to show her she's well cared-for. And do it all without complaining or acting like a martyr.

Love Stuff

176

Give your darling an Easter basket
filled with squishy marshmallow chicks,
milk chocolate bunnies, candy eggs,
and jelly beans of all colors.

Love Stuff

177

Enjoy PDA—Public Displays of Affection.
Hold hands, walk arm in arm, smooch
on the street. Who cares what anyone
else thinks?

178

Send your sweetie a new and gorgeous
nightgown (or baby dolls, satin pj's, a
silk nightshirt) once a month for a year.

Start a romantic tradition, one that reminds you of your love for each other and your ongoing romance. (One couple I know celebrates the anniversary of the day they had their first date—Halloween— by watching the Halloween parade and then going out for a great dinner.)

Love Stuff

180

Go to a polka party.

181

Go to a waltz party.

182

Go to a square dance.

Love Stuff

183

Rake leaves on a crisp, golden autumn day. When you've got the biggest pile you can possibly make, hold hands and take a running leap right onto it. Lie down and gaze up at the blue sky and puffy clouds, just as you did when you were kids.

184

Order an ice cream soda with two straws.

Love Stuff

185

See a movie at a drive-in theater. Neck like a pair of teenagers.

186

This week make a point of telling your partner what you love about her, weaving the compliments into your ordinary conversations. This is doubly effective, because you get to think about what it is you do love about her, and she gets to hear all about it.

Love Stuff

187

Love Stuff Project #5:

Get a tape recorder and spend an afternoon with each of your parents. Ask each to recount the tale of how he or she met his or her mate, fell in love, and got married. You'll have great stories to listen to over and over and to play for your kids, too.

Love Stuff

188

For the ultimate in soaring to great heights with your feet still on the ground, attend an organ recital in a towering cathedral space and be completely transported.

189

Do the housecleaning in your sexiest underwear or, if you're really hot to trot, in the nude. Make sure your guy's around to witness the proceedings—or join them!

Love Stuff

190

Write a song about your lover or your love story, or hire a professional song-writer to do it for you. Perform it for your darling in a romantic setting.

191

Rent a local hall and host a big dance party just like the ones you had in high school. Whatever your decade—'50s, '60s, '70s, '80s—be sure to play the right music, and tell everyone to come dressed in the hip clothes of the decade. Serve your favorite high school foods (everything but the Mystery Meat).

Love Stuff

192

You can't buy love, but every so often it helps to throw a little hard cash at it.

♥ Buy him a new mattress, so he'll know you think life with him is a bed of roses.

♥ Give her shares of blue-chip stock, so she'll realize you're invested in the future.

♥ Give him a new watch, so he can count the minutes until you're together again.

♥ Buy her a small ruby, so she'll know how much you prize her.

♥ Buy him a telescope, so he knows he's the sun, moon, and stars to you.

Dedicate an entire night of lovemaking to her. Do everything she desires and ask for nothing in return—until tomorrow, when you switch roles and she dedicates an entire night of lovemaking to you.

194

In these e-mail days, how often is your mailbox deliciously stuffed with snail mail? Thrill your mate by sending him all kinds of cool things for a week or two: love letters, cartoons, stories clipped from magazines, travel brochures, greeting cards, crossword puzzles, photos, a crisp twenty-dollar bill, a strip of cute stickers, coupons, poems, newspaper articles. Use different kinds of envelopes and stamps. SWAK.

Love Stuff

195

Even if you can't afford to buy a home yet, spend a weekend checking out houses for sale. Indulge in the romantic fantasy of where you'd like to live together in the future.

196

Next time he's flying for business, pack him a delicious lunch so he doesn't have to eat that weird airline food. How loving is *that?*

Love Stuff

Capture her under the mistletoe and don't let her go until you've had your fill of Christmas kisses.

Romantic Getaway:
Visit a national treasure—Cape Cod National Seashore.

199

Take your lover to a ballgame and (surprise!) reveal your romantic message in bright lights right up there on the scoreboard for all the fans to see.

200

Get in the shower together and give each other wonderful, stimulating shampoos. You can probably think of a few other wonderful, stimulating things to do, too.

Love Stuff

201

Falling asleep is an opportunity for intimacy and romance. When you're drifting off, you're vulnerable, dreamy, and (hopefully) as relaxed as you can be. So take advantage of opportunities: Nod off cuddled on your lover's lap. Let your lover fall asleep with his head on your lap. Take a nap, spooned together. Hold hands as you and your partner fall asleep.

Seems as if some people are too shy to put their loving thoughts into words—but that's *just* what they (and you) should do. Truly, it doesn't matter if your love notes are brilliantly eloquent or whimsically poetic or not, as long as you write from the heart.

Love Stuff

203

And for added impact, make your love note *look* special.

♥ Write it in calligraphy on beautiful paper.

♥ Frame it in silver or gold.

♥ Jazz it up on the computer.

♥ Trim it with glitter and sequins.

204

Volunteer together. This may not seem very romantic on the face of it, but anything you do together that feels useful, generous, meaningful, and valuable is going to make you feel even better about each other. And *that's* romantic.

205

Declare a Sadie Hawkins Day and invite your lover out for a night of dancing.

Love Stuff

206

Declare an "I Adore My Partner" Day, and pamper your beloved for twenty-four hours.

207

Buy a wildly sexy pair of undies for her and wrap them nicely. Hide the package in her briefcase when she's not looking, with a wildly sexy note telling her what the evening holds in store. You'll be hearing from her the moment she discovers it.

Love Stuff

Romantic Getaway:
Treat yourselves to a river trip down the Grand Canyon.

Spend an evening or two putting together a slide show of your latest vacation. Relive the good memories and laugh at the disasters.

Love Stuff

210

So you're a hard-nosed business type? Take your business skills and apply them to romance! This week call a meeting of the board (you and your partner), set a romantic agenda, and follow through on your program. Next week analyze where your romantic plan could be improved for better productivity, and initiate steps for making those improvements. The week after that, apply time-management techniques so you have more quality hours with your partner. At the end of the month reward yourselves with a bonus (dinner at a four-star restaurant?) when you add up the good results.

Love Stuff

211

Fun and Games #4:
Play charades, acting out the names of romantic movies or songs.

212

Borrow your kids' sleds and hit the best sledding hills in town on a sunny winter day. Be sure to take a few turns hunkered together on the same sled.

Love Stuff

213

Put on your bathing suits and run outside in a summer rain. Frolic. Chase each other. Lie on the wet grass with your faces to the sky and get thoroughly soaked.

214

Forbidden Fruit: This may (or may not!) seem a little out there to you, but why not try something you're not supposed to do? The forbidden can be exciting, and exciting can be romantic and passionate. Go to a sexy movie together. Rent an X-rated video. Read a book about seduction. Study a sex guide—and try some of the techniques!

Love Stuff

215

Don't let an anniversary sneak past you without a celebration.

- ♥ Invite your original wedding party attendants to a candlelit dinner.

- ♥ Make a reservation for two at the smartest restaurant in town.

- ♥ Have a barbecue for the whole neighborhood.

- ♥ Ask your entire family over for anniversary cake and champagne.

- ♥ Do all of the above.

216

If you went to college together, revisit your alma mater in the fall. Take a tailgate picnic to the big game. Stroll the paths of the quad and take a peek at your old dorm rooms. Get in the school spirit and feel like college sweethearts again.

217

Plan a trip to a theme park. You'll have a ball! Choose an adventure park, wildlife park, water park, Disney park, or check the Internet for lots more ideas.

Love Stuff

218

Surprise your honey with a porch swing. Have it installed when she's out for the day, then sit her down in it for a cozy, romantic ride when she gets home in the evening.

219

Make pizza together from scratch (mostly). Buy the dough ready-made at your local pizzeria, but make the sauce, grate the cheese, and prepare the toppings at home *con amore*.

Romantic Getaway:
Tour the south of France—très *fantastique.*

Get license plates with combinations of letters and numbers that have romantic meanings only you two will understand.

Love Stuff

222

Celebrate interesting holidays: On Cinco de Mayo, go to a great Mexican restaurant, preferably one with a mariachi band. On Chinese New Year, go to the Chinese district of your city and join the festivities. On Saint Patrick's Day, march in the parade, even if you're not Irish. On United Nations Day, host a potluck international supper.

Love Stuff

223

Don't buy her one beautiful bouquet—
buy two!

224

Don't buy her one box of heavenly
candy—buy two!

225

Don't buy her one exquisite diamond—
buy two!

Does your sweetie have a passion for Star Trek, Elvis, orchids, chocolate, or flamenco? Take him to the source: a Trekkie convention; Graceland; the botanic garden; Hershey, Pennsylvania; or Barcelona. He'll love you for it.

Tonight (tonight!) slip into something enticing in sleepwear, something you've never worn before—something that will throw a whole new light on the romantic proceedings.

Love Stuff

Have dinner on the back porch in the summer twilight, and linger over your coffee.

Read to each other in bed. For many folks, there's nothing more intimate.

Love Stuff

230

Sit down with each other for a session of sweet talk: Describe *every single thing* you love about each other, from hair color to toenails, every talent you admire, every attitude you like, every trait you enjoy. Fill the air with compliments and then bask in the warm glow.

231

Take an off-season vacation so the two of you will have fewer distractions and more time together in a beautiful place.

Renew your wedding vows in a cere-
mony that reflects who you are now.
It could be simple and dignified, lavish
and rollicking, or any other style. It
could be very private, overflowing with
family and friends, or somewhere in
between. You might want to repeat
your original words, write new ones,
or make them up as you go along. Any
way you do it is the right way as long
as it's *your* way.

Love Stuff

233

Love Stuff Project #6:

Together cook something sensual, spicy, sweet, succulent, or smoky—and fun to make. Bake fancy breads or cinnamon rolls. Mix up your favorite flavors in an ice cream machine. Buy a smoker and do up a batch of salmon or trout. Invent a new salsa or chutney. Yummy!

Love Stuff

Take a trip down Memory Lane: Spend a few delightful hours sorting through your collection of loose photos and putting them into gorgeous new albums.

Have you always wanted to direct a movie? Star in a movie? Get yourselves a video camera, write the script for a love story, and make the film together.

Love Stuff

236

Rent a rowboat or canoe and go out for an hour or two of lazy paddling. Being alone together in the middle of a peaceful lake is very romantic.

237

When you go off on a business trip, leave him a surprise that will keep him thinking about you and longing for your return: a love note; a book of love poetry; a valentine (even if it's June); tickets to a show for the night after you get home; a handwritten coupon for a night of love; an alluring photo of you.

238

Do something for him that he doesn't like to do for himself: Vacuum his car. Straighten out his closet. Make his dental appointment. That'll show him how much you adore him.

239

Give her an add-a-pearl necklace and add to it often.

Love Stuff

240

Pin a corsage of violets to her coat in the dead of winter.

241

Visit a romantic city—how about Venice?

242

Baby, it's cold tonight, so toss a coin—whoever loses has to get into bed first and warm it up for the other.

Love Stuff

243

Massage his feet slowly and sensuously, using strong pressure on the soles. Watch him melt.

244

Choose a restaurant to be *your* restaurant. Eat there regularly and you'll be remembered—and treated as favored customers.

Shop together for a romantic bed—a king-size bed, a bed with a canopy, a bed with beautifully carved headboard and footboard, a brass bed, an old-fashioned four-poster.

Take the Sunday paper and a picnic brunch to the park. Don't forget the mimosas (the *drink*, not the tree).

Love Stuff

247

Romance is for every day of the week, not just for weekends. Maybe you can't squeeze one of the larger romantic events into a busy weekday, but in the space of a mere ten minutes on Tuesday you could:

- ♥ send a love note by e-mail
- ♥ dash into a bookstore and pick up that mystery he's been wanting to read
- ♥ snuggle before you get out of bed in the morning
- ♥ massage her neck and back
- ♥ make him a martini

Love Stuff

248

Amuse yourselves at an amusement park. Bump around in bumper cars. Cling to each other for dear life on the roller coaster. Lose your balance on the Tilt-A-Whirl. And do not—repeat, *do not*—overlook the Tunnel of Love.

249

Instead of approaching daily chores with a scowl, view them as time you can spend together talking and joking around. Think of how much fun you have with your girlfriends when you're cleaning up after a party; think of how much fun you have with your guyfriends when you're working on the car. What's so different about washing dishes or folding laundry or shopping for groceries?

Love Stuff

250

Romantic Getaway:
If you love winter sports and miss them the rest of the year, head south in summer for skiing in Argentina or Chile.

251

Throw a Valentine's Day bash for yourselves and fifty of your closest friends at the best dance club in town.

Make a date for a cozy evening of paging through your wedding album together. Reminisce, and remember how and why you two fell for each other way back when.

Go to an estate auction and bid on an antique you both adore. Bring the romance of the past into the romance of your present—and future.

Love Stuff

254

Love stuff can be child's play. Sound silly? Maybe, but think of all the great things kids get to do: Swing on swings. Chase each other all over the house. Wrestle. Fool around in the bathtub. And paint with their fingers, which you are privileged to do on each other's naked bodies (using edible fingerpaints) because you're adults! So does child's play *still* sound silly?

Love Stuff

255

Spend a lazy summer afternoon walking through fields of wildflowers. Breathe the warm, rich scents. Listen to bees humming, birds singing, grasses rustling. Become intoxicated with the heat of the sun, then take refuge together in the cool shade of a tree.

Love Stuff

256

Listen to Books on Tape (pick great love stories!) while you're on a road trip together.

257

Share the last piece of chocolate cake. You take a bite, he takes a bite, you take a bite . . .

Make a videotape of yourself telling your darling all the things you love about him. Go into elaborate detail, and make it as personal as you can. After all, he's the only one who's going to see it, right?

Love Stuff

259

If you're the practical one in your relationship, decide to be *impractical* for a day. Forget chores and must-do's for twenty-four hours, and exercise your romantic imagination instead. Take her on a spur-of-the-moment date. Shower her with little gifts. Ignore your responsibilities to other people and pay attention only to her. See how much fun you have being spontaneous—and repeat often!

260

Tip the shampoo person at the hair salon *before* your sweetie goes for her next appointment, so the shampooer will give her a bracing scalp massage plus a great soaping.

261

Trade houses or apartments with another couple for a weekend. It can be *very* titillating to make love in a strange bed.

Love Stuff

262

Romantic Getaway:
If you love—*really* love—to walk, take a
six-day walking tour of the pure white
beaches on the southern coast of
Tasmania, an island south of Australia.

263

Take her to high tea at a fancy hotel. Eat
lots of tiny scones, miniature pastries,
itty-bitty cookies, and scrumptious
little sandwiches, with big pots of
Darjeeling. Very, very romantic.

Love Stuff

Be daring: Visit a store that sells sexy stuff and buy some things to play with—games, sex toys, costumes, videos, lotions, potions, and anything else that captures your imagination.

On the anniversary of your first date, do exactly what you did the first time around. Meet in the same place (wearing the same clothes, if possible), greet in the same way, eat the same food. Appreciate how far you've come. Recognize how far you'll go—together.

Take your darling to the ultimate event: If she loves dogs, take her to the Westminster Dog Show. If he loves gymnastics, take him to the U.S. Gymnastics Championships. If she loves high fashion, take her to Paris for the fall showings. If he loves theater, take him to the biggest Broadway hit.

Wake your lover early in the morning to invite him out to see the sunrise. Bring coffee.

Love Stuff

268

Call your sweetheart and tell her you're leaving work early to take her out on the town. Spontaneity, generosity, excitement—*that's* romance!

269

In January, celebrate New Year's Eve: Stay home together instead of going out; open a bottle of champagne and make a toast to your enduring love. Alternatively, go out to the fanciest club you can find, dressed in your snazziest clothes, and dance till dawn.

Love Stuff

270

In February, celebrate Valentine's Day: Bake him a heart-shaped cake. Give her a garnet ring. Tuck a new pair of heart-sprinkled boxers under his pillow. Buy her a chocolate cupid.

271

In March, celebrate the first day of spring: Fill the house with sunny daffodils and hot pink tulips to remind yourselves that better weather is coming. Sit down and plan your garden together.

In April, celebrate Easter: Hide small gifts and messages in hollow eggs and send her on a hunt all over the house and yard.

In May, celebrate Mother's Day: Invite both of your mothers to a gourmet dinner to thank them for producing the love of your life.

Love Stuff

274

In June, celebrate Father's Day: Take both of your fathers out on the town to thank them for doing their parts in raising the one you love.

275

In July, celebrate Independence Day: Break free from doing things exactly the same way you've always done them. Decide to be creative about your leisure time, your dinner menus, your hairdo—and especially your love life.

Love Stuff

In August, celebrate the summer: Lie in a hammock together. Go skinny-dipping. Have a picnic. Make hay while the sun shines.

In September, celebrate the first day of autumn: Head for a farm stand and buy a pumpkin for the porch. Pick apples at an orchard. Go leaf peeping. Toast your love with freshly pressed cider.

Love Stuff

278

In October, celebrate Halloween: Host a costume party, dressed as a famous pair of lovers—Romeo and Juliet, Archie and Veronica, Superman and Lois, Rhett and Scarlett.

279

In November, celebrate Thanksgiving: When dinner is over and the family has finally left, take time to tell each other how thankful you are to be together now and forever.

280

In December, celebrate Christmas: In spite of the busyness of the season, set aside one special night for the two of you. Turn the tree lights on and the room lights off and enjoy the magic from a cozy spot on the couch. Drink eggnog and reminisce about Christmases past.

Love Stuff

281

A friend told me that she loves her husband's mind, but she totally loses her head over his body, because his skin smells like fresh-baked bread. We can't all have a natural smell like warm bread or chocolate chip cookies, but we can all use fragrances that turn our lovers to jelly. Find out what scent your partner likes best and wear it.

282

Sign him up for a session or two of something he's always wanted to do but never allowed himself to try—hot-air ballooning, water skiing, white-water rafting, scuba diving, stand-up comedy class, ceramics, glass-blowing.

283

Take your mate to a concert of a singer or group you both loved way back when.

Love Stuff

284

Go to tag sales together. Buy frivolous, inexpensive things, for no good reason.

285

If you're fans of independent cinema, plan a trip around a film festival. There are many of them all over the country, and they're easily found on the Internet.

286

Buy a wireless intercom so you can chat with each other from any spot in the house.

Seeing her home safely after a date, warming up her car on a cold morning, calling him to say good night once more, checking in with him before an important job interview—small acts of care and concern are the glue that holds romance together.

♥ 288

You've heard about those lingerie
fashion shows that guys swoon over?
Maybe you've even taken a peek at one
or two. Well, now it's your turn to turn
your guy on. Buy yourself some super-
sexy lingerie (it doesn't have to be
expensive; it just has to make you feel
great) and show it off for him this very
night. Put on a little perfume while
you're at it, and a pair of strappy high
heels wouldn't hurt either. . . .

289

Challenging the mountain, the river, or the trail may be the true stuff of romance for some couples. If that's your intoxication of choice, find it on the Web and get going.

Love Stuff

290

Fun and Games #5:

Write one letter of the alphabet on each of twenty-six slips of paper and toss them in a jar. Every other week, choose one, then come up with a food, a gift, a place to go, a video, and a snack—each beginning with the chosen letter. For example, M might include: meat loaf (at a great diner), Madonna CD, marina (for a margarita by the water), *Moonstruck*, and M&M's. There's your date for that week.

Love Stuff

291

Check the newspaper for great horoscopes for your sweetheart, and send them to him. Better yet, *write* a great horoscope for him!

292

Put on soft, romantic music—vocal or instrumental, maybe some oldies from your past—and dance cheek-to-cheek with your lover in the living room.

Love Stuff

293

Have a long, intimate talk about your sex life and what you like about it—and what you'd like to add to it or change. Confide your fantasies to each other.

294

If you've taken a truly memorable vacation together, give her a gift that will remind her of it, along with a note telling her how much you treasured that time with her.

Love Stuff

Make (or buy) him a bottle of love
potion and give it
to him with a love
note attached.

Every once in a while, have a total pig-
out on your mutually favorite foods.

Love Stuff

297

Are you too much a creature of habit—or not enough of one? Make it a habit to:

♥ take walks together so you'll have time to talk

♥ eat together at least once a day

♥ go to bed at the same time (meaning simultaneously) as often as you can

♥ go to and from work together, if it's convenient

♥ all of the above

Love Stuff

298

Waste no opportunity for congratulating and praising your lover for his or her accomplishments. Send flowers, balloons, a basket of goodies, a telegram, a bottle of bubbly. E-mail your friends and relatives, announcing the good news.

299

Walk the dog together. Use the time for chatting, catching up, holding hands.

Love Stuff

300

Go to a kids' playground and do it all—swings, slides, seesaw, monkey bars.

301

Tie a bunch of pink and red balloons to your fence post to let your darling know he's welcome.

Love Stuff

302

Buy matching cashmere pullovers and wear them at the same time.

303

Start a collection of something interesting and pursue new items for it together. Silver spoons, art pottery, baseball memorabilia, inkwells, folk art—it doesn't matter what it is as long as you both enjoy the objects and the pursuit.

Love Stuff

304

Search out and visit a really special
museum, perhaps one of these:
Museum of Television and Radio, New
York, New York; San Diego Automotive
Museum, San Diego, California;
International Museum of Carousel Art,
Hood River, Oregon; Garfield Farm
Museum, St. Charles, Illinois; Buffalo
Bill Historical Center, Cody, Wyoming;
Washington Banana Museum, Auburn,
Washington.

Love Stuff

305

Have a wine-tasting party or go on a wine-tasting tour of the California wine country. Wine is definitely romantic.

306

On a dark and starry night, drive your partner to the local make-out spot, put on a CD, and hug and kiss till dawn.

Love Stuff

307

Get a roll of white paper and a stack of fat felt-tip markers at the art supply store, and (together) write your love story in words and pictures. Start with your first meeting and work your way up in time to the present day. Be frivolous and silly, loving and gooey, frisky and saucy. Put it all down on paper, and have a good time doing it!

308

Go to a chocolate shop and buy one of everything. Taste-test together.

309

Go to a department store and try out the scents together—hers *and* his.

310

Go to a toy store and buy a new board game to play together.

Love Stuff

311

Surprise your mate in the dark days of winter: After he leaves for work, have lots of colored lights strung on and around your home. What a romantic sight for him to see when he pulls up to the house that night . . .

312

Rent a movie theater for a night for just the two of you, to watch your favorite romantic film in total privacy. Don't forget the champagne and popcorn.

Love Stuff

313

Get your hair cut at the same unisex salon, at the same time, sitting in adjacent chairs.

314

Read your favorite children's books to each other, aloud.

315

Love Stuff Project #7:
Knit him a sweater, but let him pick out the yarn.

Love Stuff

316

Have Happy Hour at home, together, instead of at the local pub. Kick back and treat yourselves to your favorite drinks and snacks. Bonus: No driving home when Happy Hour's over.

317

Romantic Getaway:
Take a canoe out at sunset, on String Lake in Grand Teton National Park. Have a picnic dinner when you reach the end of the lake.

How does your garden grow? Visit a botanic garden, fragrance garden, healing garden, roof garden, rock garden, historic garden—and luxuriate in the scents and sights.

Wake her in the middle of the night to make love. (But *not* if she's had an exhausting day at the office or been up for three nights straight with a sick child.)

Love Stuff

320

Have private jokes, phrases, and signals that only you two understand and that set you laughing or blushing no matter who else is around.

321

Do you groan inwardly at the approach of the weekend? Does it loom as a forty-eight-hour nonstop round of chores, errands, and catch-up? Well, that requires an immediate change of thinking. Let no weekend pass without your spending some time together doing *something* you both enjoy.

Love Stuff

Speak in the language of flowers by sending her:

- ♥ tulips, to tell her she's a perfect lover
- ♥ anemones, for anticipation
- ♥ daisies, to tell her of your loyal love
- ♥ calla lilies, to remind her she's beautiful
- ♥ forget-me-nots, for true love

Love Stuff

Throw the party of your dreams, together. Would it be an all-day open house in your backyard? A lantern-lit evening on your patio? A New Year's Eve extravaganza? A formal dinner? A swim-fest at the local beach? Whatever your preference, make it memorable.

Fun and Games #6:
Get wild and crazy: Have a food fight, a water fight, or a pillow fight.

Love Stuff

325

If you're strapped for cash, a (romantic) splurge can rescue you before your relationship turns into a financial battlefield. Don't blow the very last of your bank account, but do take yourselves out to a good dinner and a movie or show. Relax and enjoy it—lift your spirits tonight so that tomorrow you return to your real lives with renewed energy and love.

Love Stuff

326

Give each other facials and make them very sensual experiences.

327

Go to an astrologer or fortune-teller together and learn about your future. It doesn't matter if you don't believe in all that—it's just for fun!

If you both love dogs: Enter your pup in a dog show. March in a parade with your beloved pooch. Visit pet shops and coo over the puppies. Read books on your favorite breed. Plan a vacation around places that *welcome* dogs. See films that feature dogs: *Lassie Come Home*; *As Good as It Gets*; *Turner and Hooch*. Check in on Snoopy.

Love Stuff

329

If you both love cats: Grow catnip. Take your mouser to the country for the weekend. Build or buy a simple scratching post or an elaborate kitty penthouse with a couple of levels. Take your cat to the annual Blessing of the Animals at church. See *Harry and Tonto*. Read *archy and mehitabel* by Don Marquis. Keep up with Garfield.

Love Stuff

330

If you both love horses: Go to the races. Take riding lessons. Take a pack trip on horseback. Spend a vacation at a horse ranch. See *National Velvet*, *The Black Stallion*, *The Black Stallion Returns*, *Black Beauty*, *The Horse Whisperer*, *Seabiscuit*. Ride in a horse-drawn carriage. Watch reruns of *Mr. Ed*.

331

Take a massage class—together.

Love Stuff

332

On a hot summer day, put on your bathing suits and take a big wedge of ice-cold watermelon out to the back yard. Gobble up the melon, get deliciously sticky, and then rinse off under the garden sprinkler.

333

Write love letters in code.

Let your partner brush or comb your hair.

Tell each other your feelings from A to Z: A, you Adore each other; B, you're the Best thing that's happened to each other; C, you'll Care for each other forever; and so on, all the way to Z. (Okay, you may skip X!)

Love Stuff

336

Give her a big welcome when she
returns from a business trip: String a
"Welcome Home" banner across the
porch. Carry her luggage up to the
bedroom. Offer to run a hot bath for
her. Listen to her stories about the trip.
Have a wonderful meal waiting, along
with a great bottle of wine. Above all,
greet her with a double dose of hugs
and kisses to show her how much you
missed her.

Love Stuff

337

Love Stuff Project #8:
Stencil the four walls of your favorite room together. Try a hearts-and-flowers theme.

338

Take a pinup-style photo of yourself and leave it in his shirt pocket.

339

Give your lover the most impractical gift you can think of.

Love Stuff

340

Take a sauna together, to get all steamed up.

341

Surprise him or her with a kid-free dinner tonight. Send the children out with a babysitter or over to Grandma and Grandpa's for at least three hours so you can have a quiet, intimate dinner for two. Candles, wine, flowers, the best china. Oh, yes, and food, too . . .

342

Spend an afternoon at the zoo.

Spend an afternoon
at the aquarium.

Buy the biggest, most complicated
jigsaw puzzle you can find, and do it
together. Plan a nifty reward for the day
you finish it.

If "your" song happens to be a popular
one, make a tape or CD of a dozen different singers singing it. Don't forget the
French, Spanish, and Japanese versions!

Love Stuff

346

Home movies are your personal history. Spend time together watching them and remembering all the fun you've had over the years.

347

Blow the fuses (well, flip the circuit breaker switches or whatever it takes) and spend an evening in candlelight. No TV, no videos, no stereo, no computer, no power tools, no sewing machine—nothing but the two of you in the semi-dark. What can you do to amuse yourselves? You'll think of something.

Love Stuff

❤ **348**

Turn his birthday into a birthweek: On the actual day, give him his gifts and make a special dinner for him. On each subsequent day, honor his birthday with a small or large celebration:

Day 2: Send flowers to his office.

Day 3: Invite his best friend over for dinner.

Day 4: Make him a brown bag lunch, including a frosted birthday cupcake.

Love Stuff

Day 5: Take him to an event—ball game, concert, theater, whatever he enjoys.

Day 6: Decorate the front door with a huge bunch of birthday balloons.

Day 7: This is the big one—throw him a surprise party!

349

Instead of drowsing off after making love, bring on some special treats: chilled white wine, juicy cherries or strawberries, fancy chocolates, tiny pastries. Or go in the opposite flavor direction: tangy olives, creamy brie cheese, pâté, caviar, champagne.

Love Stuff

350

Romantic Getaway:
Walk or bike through Tuscany, stopping
often to eat, drink, and enjoy the scenery.

351

Take a bicycle-trip-for-two, for a day,
a weekend, or even longer. Check out
websites targeted at casual or adven-
turous cyclers and see what suggestions they have to offer.

Love Stuff

352

Intimacy is crucial to romance, so try this: Snuggle up spoon-style in a hammock or lounge chair, on the couch or on the bed—and breathe together. Concentrate on allowing the rhythm of your breathing to match his or allowing his to match yours. Now let your mind go, and float together in a peaceful place.

Love Stuff

353

Any night can be party night. Serve some party food on any ordinary Monday-through-Thursday—caviar on toast points, smoked mussels, creamy Camembert, macadamia nuts, cupcakes, petits fours—and get into a party spirit.

354

Fun and Games #7:
Play Truth or Dare.

355

Take your sweetheart to a magic show, for a magical night of romance.

Love Stuff

356

Chop your own Christmas tree at a tree farm. Decorate it together.

357

Indulge in movie snacks—popcorn, candy, nachos, and so on—at *home*, with a video.

358

Wear white T-shirts (with *nothing* underneath) while you're out washing the car (or the siding, windows, whatever) and be sure you both get soaking wet . . . just to cool off, of course.

Here's a three-part romantic assignment: First, give your sweetheart a video camcorder for a birthday or holiday. Second, encourage him to use it to record the happy events of your life. Third, cuddle up together and watch the replays.

On the first of every month, e-mail him a short list of possible dates, outings, fun things to do. Ask him to pick one (or more) and name the day he wants to do it. Write it into your calendar and hold him to it.

Love Stuff

361

Go on a Great Cookie Hunt together.
Start at one end of town and buy at
least three cookies in every bakery you
can find. Taste, taste, taste to find the
absolutely most delicious. (Remember
the winner next time you want to buy
your darling a sweet treat.)

362

Skip Ye Same Olde Motel and opt for
romance instead: Before your next trip,
do a little research and find a charming
bed-and-breakfast or small hotel to
stay in.

363

Go to the

♥ football game

♥ car show

♥ comedy club

♥ high school reunion

♥ hardware store

with him, and act as if you're enjoying yourself.

Go to the

- ♥ mushy movie
- ♥ garden show
- ♥ modern dance performance
- ♥ family reunion
- ♥ shoe store

with her, and act as if you're enjoying
yourself.

Love Stuff

365

Fun and Games #8:
Arm wrestle. Two out of three wins. Winner gets whatever winner wants, romantically speaking.

366

Create a gigantic, overstuffed Dagwood sandwich and share it.

367

Take a picnic up into your kids' tree house. But no kids allowed!

Love Stuff

368

Have you heard of the Mile-High Club? Well, don't tell anyone, but it's a "club" for couples who have made love in those itsy-bitsy restrooms on airplanes. Care to join?

369

Here's a cool way to do Saturday night: Meet for drinks at a lively bar (*don't fill up on peanuts*). Move on to a nice restaurant for dinner, but don't have dessert. Take a stroll and wind up at a lovely café for dessert and coffee. Changing venues multiplies your pleasure.

370

If you happen to be downtown at just the time he leaves work, surprise your guy at the train station or at his car and make the trip home together.

371

On a big piece of paper, draw the floor plans for your dream house. Spare no (imaginary) expense; put in absolutely everything you want. After all, it's just a dream—for now.

Love Stuff

372

Romantic Getaway:

See the Taj Mahal, the greatest shrine to love and romance ever built.

373

Have a private film festival. Take out five videos or DVDs with a theme. Here are some possibilities: films of a favorite actor; films by a favorite director; films on a favorite topic; action or suspense films; comedies; films of a particular decade; foreign films. Watch all the films in one sitting . . . okay, two sittings, with breaks.

Love Stuff

Give him your heart in the form of
heart-shaped sugar cookies, a love
note on a heart-shaped paper doily,
a message written in a lipstick heart
on the bathroom mirror, or a teeny
heart-shaped tattoo (temporary or
permanent) on *you*—in a spot that only
he gets to see.

Love Stuff

375

Give her your heart in the form of chocolates in a heart-shaped box, heart-shaped earrings, a love note chalked in a heart on her paved driveway, or a teeny heart-shaped tattoo (temporary or permanent) someplace on *you*—in a spot that only *she* gets to see.

Love Stuff

376

Does your community sponsor summer band concerts or theater in the park under the stars? If it does, don't miss these performances. Take a blanket and a delicious picnic and settle in for a romantic evening.

377

See the U.S.A. together—visit every state in the union!

Love Stuff

378

If you love to go camping, make it your business to camp out in great national parks.

379

Take him to places he's never (or rarely) been: a lingerie store, bath and body shop, jewelry store. Try things on. Sniff. Admire. Hint.

380

Go to a karaoke bar, get up there at the mike, and belt out a song to your beloved.

Love Stuff

381

Make him #1 on your automatic dialer; make her #1 on your automatic dialer.

382

Are you and your mate looking for a dramatic way to have fun? Join the local amateur theater group. Few things are more romantic than the world of the theater—the thrill of putting on a play—whether you're onstage or backstage.

Love Stuff

383

Late on Saturday night, take a stroll together to buy the Sunday paper. Then you won't have to get out of bed on Sunday morning.

384

Take him to a World Series game and go all the way—team cap and T-shirt, hot dogs, Cracker Jacks, the works.

Sure, you're busy all day, but can you find a minute or two tonight to change out of your baggy sweats into pants and a pretty jersey? Can you find one more minute to blow-dry a little life into your hair and gloss your lips? That extra bit of effort says to your partner that you don't take him for granted.

Love Stuff

386

Throughout the year, buy small gifts for your darling and stash them away—but not for too long. Surprise him with one of the gifts whenever there's a fitting occasion, like when the car breaks down or the boss is surly or it's been raining for a week.

387

More on gifts: Every so often, present your partner with a gift of a little (or a lot of) cash to spend any way she likes. She'll love you for it.

Love Stuff

388

Send not one but ten (or more!) valentines. Sign them in a variety of romantic ways: From Your Secret Admirer, With Love from You-Know-Who, From the One Who Adores You, For My Darling Tootsie-Wootsie (or whatever secret nickname makes her tingle).

389

Play kissing games.

Love Stuff

390

Take a bath together.

391

Let him shave your legs. Let her shave your face. Take your time and get into the sensuality of the experience.

Love Stuff

Experiment with new massage oil, scented lotions, bath gel, fragrant powder—something to wake up your senses.

Romantic Getaway:
Hop down to Nashville for the Grand Ole Opry. Hoot, holler, and have a great time.

Love Stuff

394

Lose yourselves in a deep, mesmerizing interlude—gazing at the flames in the fireplace, watching the motion of ocean waves, listening to soothing music or sounds, swinging gently in a hammock.

395

Transfer the proceedings to the floor: Scatter big soft pillows on the floor in front of the fireplace (maybe spread a fluffy quilt there, too) and get comfortable for a couple of hours.

Love Stuff

396

Initiate a little rooftop romance—with a blanket, some wine, and a million stars.

397

Rent an apartment in Paris, Rome, or Madrid for a week and pretend you live there.

398

Dress in your whites and play croquet on the lawn. Drink iced tea and eat cucumber sandwiches.

Love Stuff

399

When she goes off on a business trip, send flowers, a card, a love letter, or any other goody to her hotel to greet her when she arrives.

400

When he goes off on a business trip, burn him a CD to play on the airplane: Make a mix of his favorite romantic songs—and a few of yours, too.

Love Stuff

401

Fun and Games #9:
On slips of paper write all the romantic things you'd like to do with your sweet-heart. (Be bold—"romantic" might include passionate and sexy as well as sweet and innocent.) Have your honey do the same. Put the slips into two jars—one for each of you—and take turns picking and doing.

Love Stuff

402

Slice juicy peaches into flutes of champagne; eat the peaches with your fingers, then drink the champagne. Dip strawberries into melted chocolate and feed them to each other.

403

Next time you go out for dinner, order something that can only be made for two.

Love Stuff

404

Sprinkle your bed with fresh or silk rose petals. Light a rose-scented candle, too.

405

Do you have a bad case of SAD— Seasonal Affective Disorder? In other words, have winter and the lack of sunshine got you down and depressed? Nobody feels romantic while depressed, so take off for a refresher in warmer, lighter climes.

Love Stuff

406

Give your sweetie a dozen prepaid phone cards so he can call you as much as he wants when he can't be with you.

407

Romantic Getaway:
Celebrate Christmas at Deer Lodge in Lake Louise, Alberta. Go for the giant Christmas tree, the delicious eggnog, the gorgeous scenery, and the skiing.

Care and concern are inextricably linked to romance. How do you show your lover that you care? Perhaps your way is to

♥ bring her breakfast in bed

♥ massage his shoulders when he's tired and tense

♥ listen attentively to whatever is troubling her

♥ whisk him away for a much-needed afternoon or day of relaxation

♥ all of the above

Love Stuff

409

Do something romantic on New Year's *Day*, to get the year off to a great loving start.

410

What's her favorite romantic movie? Give her a DVD or videotape of it— then make a gigantic bowl of popcorn and watch the film with her.

Love Stuff

411

If you play the piano or guitar, sit your lover down and treat him to a miniconcert of romantic songs or songs that are meaningful to the two of you.

412

In the Northeast, visit one of the wonderful summer music festivals— Caramoor or Glimmerglass, Jacob's Pillow or Tanglewood. (Even the names are romantic.)

413

Take your guy to a slap-up black-tie charity affair. Have a glass of champagne and take a spin around the dance floor, and you'll be feeling generous, glamorous, sophisticated, elegant, and very romantic indeed.

414

For a no-fuss romantic holiday, check into a great hotel in your own city for the weekend. Do all the fun stuff your town has to offer.

Love Stuff

♥ 415

Your love story is special, isn't it? It's certainly special to *you*, so celebrate it in a way that brings it back all over again. If you fell in love while you were dancing to "Moon River," rent the DVD or video of *Breakfast at Tiffany's*. If you found each other on a cruise, go for a moonlight boat ride. If you flipped for each other way back in high school, return to your hometown for a nostalgic visit.

Love Stuff

416

Go to the library together, but this time you pick out five books for *him* and have him pick out five books for you. Fiction, biographies, cookbooks, travel books, books of photographs— be inventive. Expand your worlds.

417

Love Stuff Project #9:
Build a pretty birdhouse together. Paint it in bright colors, set it out in the yard, and wait for surprises.

Love Stuff

418

Romantic Getaway:
See the Brooklyn Botanic Garden in
late spring, for a stunning display of
lilacs, wisteria, and roses, and the
Japanese garden, too.

419

Buy a beautiful hope chest and fill it
together.

Love Stuff

Dance for your lover. Be slinky, be wild, be seductive. He'll love it.

Set his heart aflame: Take him for a spin in a fire engine.

Don't look now, but wouldn't you both love to shed your clothes in a sunny (secluded) meadow? Go ahead and do it!

Love Stuff

423

Don't forget small acts of romance-
from-a-slight-distance:

- ♥ E-mail a love note.

- ♥ Mail a funny card.

- ♥ Send a love quiz clipped from a
  magazine.

- ♥ Drop a "miss you" missive in the
  in-box.

- ♥ Forward a sexy story downloaded
  from the Internet.

Love Stuff

424

Write down, in descending order of priority, the ten things each of you would most like to do with the other. Your list can include everything from the sublime to the ridiculous. Exchange lists and make all of it happen.

425

If she's having a bad-hair day, mess up your own hair so she won't feel so bad.

Love Stuff

426

Join a country club and participate in *everything*—tennis, golf, swimming, parties, and especially those romantic dances in the clubhouse or on the patio.

427

When one or both of you have been working hard and can't face the thought of making dinner or going out, stop off at your favorite restaurant for a complete take-home meal. Call ahead so the food will be ready and waiting when you dash in to pick it up.

Love Stuff

428

Buy thick, plush towels for your baths and luxuriate in the luscious softness.

429

Make your bed with satin sheets and see where *that* takes you.

430

Fun and Games #10:
Tickle each other until you're helpless with laughter.

Love Stuff

Have a real summer beach picnic—the old-fashioned kind, with clams and mussels and lobsters cooked over campfires. Serve sweet corn and plates of juicy sliced tomatoes, and finish up with marshmallows toasted over the dying embers.

Go to an appropriate restaurant for an evening of planning your next vacation together—Japanese for Japan, Italian for Italy, you get the idea—and get *excited* about it.

Love Stuff

Build an extravagant sand castle
together. Decorate it
with shells and
beach glass.

Romantic Getaway:
Fly to Vladivostok or Beijing and board
the Trans-Siberian Railway for the long
exotic ride to Helsinki.

Love Stuff

435

If you're the stay-at-home one (a busy mom, freelancer, home office worker), make your partner's homecoming a little more romantic once or twice a week, to set the mood for the rest of the evening. Give this six-step program a try:

1. Change your clothes—this helps *you* get into the mood.
2. Straighten the living room—don't *clean* it, just *straighten* it.
3. Send the kids to the playroom or over to Grandma's.

Love Stuff

4. Put on some music you and your mate both like. Set the dining table for two.
5. Tackle dinner in the simplest possible way—take-out or something microwavable.
6. Pour yourself a glass of wine and give yourself a few minutes to unwind.

436

For an extra helping of intimacy and coziness, turn down the lights in the dining room, living room, bedroom. See how differently you both behave when bright light is dimmed.

Love Stuff

437

Pick a "Not-Our-Anniversary Day" and on that day give *yourselves* a big gift you've been craving and saving for: a sailboat, a new sound system, a washer-dryer, a roof garden, a summer cottage, a backyard pool, a pool table, a purebred puppy, a set of elegant china, a Jacuzzi.

438

Turn your van or RV into a rolling love nest, complete with cushy mattress, pillows, low lighting, the works.

Love Stuff

439

Surprise her with a matching set of the sexiest undies and bra you can find. Insist that she model them for you that very night.

440

Declare a Pajama Day: Stay in your pj's, and give yourselves permission to do no work, eat only silly little meals, lie around like lazy pussycats, catch up on *very light* reading, watch TV, cuddle, listen to music, chat, snuggle, yawn, and generally do nothing. Go to sleep early and dream sweet dreams.

Dress up as Santa, sit her on your lap, and find out what she *really* wants for Christmas. (And then give it to her, of course.)

Flirt with each other as if you had just met.

Love Stuff

443

Watch the film *The Full Monty* together.

444

Celebrate the winter solstice—the longest night of the year—with a private party for the two of you.

445

Celebrate the summer solstice—the longest day of the year—by staying awake till dawn and singing the sun up.

446

Romantic Getaway:
Go to extremes—Land's End, the
extreme tip of England, to gaze across
the Atlantic and have cream teas.

447

Viewing the transcendently beautiful
cherry blossoms—in your hometown, in
Washington, D.C., or even in Japan—is a
transcendently romantic thing to do.

448

Give her a lovely bud vase and keep it filled with a new flower every other day.

449

Give her a charm bracelet and add a new charm on every special romantic occasion.

450

Give her a portable CD player and present her with a new CD every month.

Love Stuff

451

Buy lottery tickets together
and watch the evening
news to see if
you've won.

452

If you two are in a phase in which it's
impossible to find time together,
alone—it's the end of the school year,
it's the week before sales meeting, it's
holiday season—lunch à deux may be
the only seventy-five minutes you can
carve out. Grab them.

Love Stuff

453

Fun and Games #11:
Treat yourselves to a few rounds of miniature golf.

454

Send him to camp for a week—baseball, tennis, music, or any other grown-ups' camp he'd love. Pick him up on the last day and whisk him off to a country inn for a couple of days of getting reacquainted.

Love Stuff

455

Instant Gratification is the name of the *Love Stuff* game, at least some of the time. I.G. may mean jumping into the car and hitting the road or grabbing your coats and heading for a movie. It may mean tearing off your clothes and tumbling into bed. The point is that *at least some of the time* it's far more important to have fun with your partner than it is to do laundry or clean the leaves out of the gutters. Get spontaneous! Now!

Love Stuff

456

Make him a whole dinner of his favorite hors d'oeuvres.

457

Have your handwriting analyzed, to find out just how romantic you and your partner really are.

458

Is he a dessert-lover? How about you for dessert, topped here and there with dabs of whipped cream?

Love Stuff

459

Deck yourself out in a romantic dress—
a fantasy number that will put your guy
in a fantasy mood.

460

If your office holds big holiday parties
at which "significant others" are welcome, invite your partner and intro-
duce him proudly. After all, he supports
your career, doesn't he? Don't your
officemates deserve to meet your
wonderful guy?

Love Stuff

461

Renew yourselves on the first of every month:

- ♥ Try a new restaurant.
- ♥ Try a new dance step.
- ♥ Try a new compliment.
- ♥ Try a new kiss.
- ♥ Try one of the suggestions in this book.

Love Stuff

Buy a pair of silk pajamas—the top is for you and the bottom is for him.

Toss a red scarf over the night-table lamp to give the bedroom a delicious glow.

Love Stuff

464

Read your lover a steamy chapter from an erotic novel.

465

Spring is the time when *everyone's* fancy lightly turns to thoughts of love, so take a spring break for romance: Head south, just the way the college kids do, and have a wild time.

466

Give your partner a sponge bath—not when she's sick in bed, but when she's feeling perfectly fine.

467

Just as choosing the *right* gift is the essence of gift giving, planning the *right* activity is the essence of romance. If it's Friday and your mate is totally bushed after a hard week, painting the town red is probably not the right activity for tonight. Neither is another quiet night at home if she's been stuck in the house all week. Think it through: What's the best romantic suggestion you can make for the particular situation you two are in right now?

Love Stuff

Fun and Games #12:
Pretend you're stranded in a mountain cabin or on a desert island for a night. What would you do?

Got insomnia? Don't fight it! Instead, put on some romantic music, light a few candles, and make love. Who cares if you're exhausted in the morning? Think of the memories!

Love Stuff

470

Take a ferry ride in the moonlight.

471

Walk across a bridge at sunset.

472

Romantic Getaway:
Explore Cape May, New Jersey, with its Victorian homes and gaslit streets, its many antique stores—and the Atlantic Ocean, too.

Love Stuff

473

Make a garden for her. Plant it with her favorite flowers.

474

Bake his favorite cookies and tell him he doesn't have to share a single one.

475

Order a wedding cake— for your next anniversary.

Maybe you've never played the lottery, but what if you did and you won a million dollars? Tell your partner what you'd do for *him* if you had a million dollars, and then let him tell you what he'd do for *you*.

Go to a restaurant or bar with a great jukebox and play all your favorite romantic tunes.

Love Stuff

478

Time for some romantic exercise: Get those lips moving with kisses. Get those hands moving with loving touches. Get those arms moving with hugs.

479

Try an activity the two of you have never done before or haven't done since you were kids: ice skating, bowling, Ping-Pong, video arcade games, square dancing, browsing through a toy store. Do something fun and new *together*.

Love Stuff

480

If you two are casual, spur-of-the-moment types, get into the day-of-the-performance ticket loop. Lots of theaters, symphonies, dance troupes, and other groups sell half-price tickets just before their performances. Spontaneity and serendipity are part of romance!

481

Tell your secrets and your secret feelings to each other—in the dark.

Love Stuff

482

Confide your dreams to each other each morning.

483

If you both love the Great Outdoors but you never have enough time to enjoy it, plan a special day or week for getting out there. Try hiking in a state park, bird-watching at dawn, canoeing on a glassy lake, snorkeling off the shore of an exotic island, bicycling over rolling hills. Rediscover nature—and each other.

Love Stuff

484

Hit a jazz club to hear your favorite trio, group, or cutting-edge performer.

485

On Christmas Eve, dress warmly and stroll arm-in-arm through your neighborhood to see all the lights and decorations on your neighbors' homes. Enjoy the romance of Christmas.

Love Stuff

486

You've heard that old expression, "Absence makes the heart grow fonder," haven't you? When romance is at a low ebb, take a time-out. Kiss your partner good-bye and leave home for a day or two. Visit a friend, your sister, or your college roommate for forty-eight hours. Your guy will miss you while you're gone. You'll miss him, too, and reunion will be sweet!

Invite your darling to a scary, scary movie—and be her romantic hero by holding her tight and protecting her when she quakes with fear.

Fun and Games #13:
Play strip poker. Or strip chess. Or strip checkers.

Indulge her: Do something (with her) that she's always wanted you to do, something you've always refused to do. Next week, she can do the same for you.

No matter how you say it, it's still romance: *Woo* her with sweet words. *Court* her with flowers. *Flirt* with him until he melts. *Pursue* her with ardor. *Dally* with her all night.

491

Couch potatoes have earned a bad rep, but couch potatoing can be a total treat on a night when all you want to do is put up your feet and vegetate. Grab a bag of chips, turn on your favorite show, and wrap up together in an afghan like a pair of peas in a pod.

492

Don't let those frequent-flier miles add up forever: Take her on a romantic trip ASAP.

Love Stuff

493

Let her drive your Corvette. No holds barred.

494

Promise to throw sensational parties for each other on marker birthdays.

495

Some romantic gifts are *never* (well, rarely) wrong: champagne, chocolates, roses, diamonds, sports cars, exotic vacations.

496

Trade moms for a day: You take his mom out for shopping, movies, museums, lunch, dinner—whatever she enjoys— and he takes yours. This gives you and Mom a chance to talk nonstop about your darling (her child), and moms sure love to do that!

497

Make up passionate, loving nicknames for each other. Use them *only* in private.

Love Stuff

498

Hot tub. Together. No bathing suits. Need we say more?

499

Leave a trail of confetti hearts from your front door to your bedroom door, and be waiting there for him in your sexiest robe. (What's a little confetti clean-up compared to the delight of a romantic adventure?)

500

Romance is *not hard*. Romance is *easy*, because it's there in every one of us in some form or another. The trick is finding the romantic overlap between you. Maybe you think a camping trip is romantic and she doesn't; maybe she thinks a black-tie affair is romantic and you don't. But maybe you *both* think

♥ a moonlight boat trip around the island
♥ a picnic
♥ a trip to Paris
♥ a walk in the woods
♥ a blues guitar concert

are romantic and thrilling. Skip the camping and the black tie and go for the five things you agree on.

Love Stuff

501

Even if you hate the way it looks in the living room, buy him a lounger if that's what will make him happy.

502

Tell each other your most secret secrets. Swear you'll never repeat them to a soul, and keep your promise.

503

Go to a big party and spend the evening *together*, an island of love in a sea of strangers.

Love Stuff

504

Take piano lessons together and learn to play romantic duets.

505

Do the Saturday crossword together. In bed.

Love Stuff

506

Love Stuff Project #10:
Create a small lovers' knot garden in
the backyard. Ask a garden expert to
help you choose herbs or shrubs that
can be pruned into neat, compact little
hedges. Make your garden grow, along
with your love.

Love Stuff

507

Try some sexy new tricks to give a boost to your romance:

- ♥ Wear a garter belt and stockings.
- ♥ Wear a short, short skirt and bend over often.
- ♥ Go braless tonight, under a V-neck jersey.

Love Stuff

And a few more tricks, for *him* to try:

- ♥ Undress down to bikini briefs and parade around casually.
- ♥ Hop in the shower before bed, and then ask your lady to dry you off.
- ♥ Blindfold your partner and *then* make love to her.

Write out a love poem (yours or another poet's) and leave it on his pillow.

Love Stuff

510

Romantic gifts are *wonderful*, but the gift of time and attention is even better. Give each other as much as you can, as often as you can. It may not be easy (so many demands on our time and attention) but it's the most important thing you can do for yourselves.

511

Romantic Getaway:
Disappear to an island for a week. Try Nantucket, Sanibel, Menorca, Madagascar, Sardinia, Puerto Rico, or even Manhattan!

Love Stuff

512

Buy her the most adorable stuffed animal you can find.

513

Write her the most loving note you can dream up.

514

Give her the most delicious kiss you can invent.

Love Stuff

515

Lazy Sundays are a gift to lovers. Sleep late. Make love. Prepare breakfast and take it back to bed with you. Read the Sunday paper. Make love again. Nap. Consider getting up, but don't. Have a snack. Watch a great old video. Read more of the paper. Order Chinese food for dinner (keep those jammies on) and go back to bed. Make love *again*. Crash.